NH Rocks That Rock

Also by Dan Szczesny

The Adventures of Buffalo and Tough Cookie
(BONDCLIFF BOOKS, 2013)

*The Nepal Chronicles: Marriage, Mountains
and Momos in the Highest Place on Earth*
(HOBBLEBUSH BOOKS, 2014)

Sing and Other Short Stories
(HOBBLEBUSH BOOKS, 2015)

Mosquito Rain: Alaskan Travel Essays
(FOLDED WORD, 2016)

Invincible One, Poems
(EKP BOOKS, 2017)

*The White Mountain: Rediscovering
Mount Washington's Hidden Culture*
(HOBBLEBUSH BOOKS, 2018)

You and Me: Reflections on Becoming Your Dad
(HOBBLEBUSH BOOKS, 2020)

NH ROCKS THAT ROCK

An Adventure Guide to Twenty-Five
Famous Boulders of the Granite State

Uma & Dan Szczesny

HOBBLEBUSH BOOKS
Concord, New Hampshire

Copyright © 2021 by Uma and Dan Szczesny

All rights reserved. No part of this work may be used or reproduced in any manner whatsoever without written permission from the publisher, except in the case of brief quotations embodied in critical articles and reviews.

This book is made possible with the help of a grant from the New Hampshire State Council on the Arts.

Composed in Calluna and Calluna Sans at Hobblebush Books
Cover concept by Dan Szczesny (danszczesny.com)

Printed in the United States of America

ISBN: 978-1-939449-16-0

Due to changes in conditions, weather, construction, and property ownership, use of the information in this field guide is at the sole risk of the user.

HOBBLEBUSH BOOKS
PO Box 1285
Concord, NH 03302
www.hobblebush.com

To Meenakshi, our rock

Contents

INTRODUCTION 3

Drive-Ups
   Big Bertha 8
   Boise Rock 10
   Chicken Farmer Rock 12
   Indian Kitty Rocks 14
   Madison Boulder 16
   Nessie's Humps 18
   Old Man of the Valley 20
   Ordination Rock 22
   The Train/Londonderry Boulder 24
   Vessel Rock 26

Short Hikes
   Balance Rock 30
   The BOB 32
   Boulder Natural Area 34
   Buffalo Rock 36
   Dog Rock 38
   Elephant Head Rock 40
   Frog Rock 42
   Indian Rock 44
   Sheep (Dog) Rock 46
   TMNT Rock 48

Optional Hikes/Drive-Ups
   Big Rock Caves 53
   Eunice "Goody" Cole Memorial Stone 54
   Gilfillan Rock 55
   Glen Boulder 56
   Goodrich Rock 57
   Humongous Boulder, Stoddard Rocks 58
   Monkey Rock 59
   Old Man of Keene 60
   Papoose Rock 61
   Playscape Playground 62

Quimby's Pillow   63
  Sarcophagus   64
  Tippin' Rock   65
  T-Rex Rock   66
  Underhill's Chair   67
  Wolf Rock   68

BIBLIOGRAPHY   69
ACKNOWLEDGMENTS   70
ABOUT THE AUTHORS   72
ROCKS THAT ROCK 25 PROGRESS LIST   73

NH Rocks That Rock

Introduction

New Hampshire loves its rocks.

The Granite State's nickname actually comes from a preponderance of nineteenth-century quarries, though the casual visitor wouldn't know it from how many famous, historic, named or identified rocks and boulders there are all across the state.

From the ocean to the south to the river valley and the grand White Mountains up north, the state is full of boulders with eccentric names—the Old Man of the Valley, Nessie's Humps, Big Bertha, T-Rex, Boise Rock, Glen Boulder, and the BOB, to name a few. Stop by Elephant, Dog, Frog, Sheep, Monkey and Wolf rocks. Take a ferry to the Isle of Shoals for Underhill's Chair. And take a moment to puzzle out the state's greatest love story—the Chicken Farmer I Still Love You Rock.

Some are boulders. Some are glacier erratics. Some are cleaved from cliffs and mountain walls. Others just happened to be in places of historic importance and have been labeled through time. Some are monuments to people or events. A few have signs, while many you'll have to search for. Some are brand new. A few have been on the New Hampshire map since before New Hampshire was New Hampshire.

One weighs more than 5,000 tons and is one of the largest glacier erratics in North America. You can't miss Madison Boulder.

But before we get into specifics, here's some definitions for the budding geologists among you. Let's start with this—what the heck is a rock anyway?

Well, geologists use a unit of measurement called the Udden-Wentworth scale to measure granular material, and this includes those things—pebbles, stones, boulders—that we know as rocks.

A boulder, generally speaking, is a rock fragment greater than 10.1 inches or more in size. A cobble is a rock 2.5 to ten inches, while a pebble falls on the scale in the area of 0.16 to 2.5 inches large. Beyond that, it gets tricky. A glacier erratic can be any type or size rock, but deposited by glacier ice outside its native location.

An aside: The word erratic is derived from the Latin, *errare*, which means *to wander*. A wandering rock. I like that very much.

Anyway, clastic rocks are composed of fragments of pre-existing minerals and rock. Conglomerates, meanwhile, are clastic rocks composed mostly of gravel sized sediments of other types of rocks. Fanglomerates are mostly gravel.

And a stone is basically what the English call rocks.

Finally, what of New Hampshire? Well, as I mentioned above, our bedrock is not Granite. In fact, our nickname really ought to be the Schist State, but I'm guessing that would cause too many jokes from middle school kids. Want an example of schist? Try the summit of Mount Washington. Want to see some granite? Look up at Cannon Cliff as you're passing through Franconia Notch State Park.

But as my daughter would remind me, just enjoy the rocks daddy. So that's what we'll do.

A few months ago, during a short hike out to Frog Rock in New Boston, my six-year-old daughter asked me what other rocks were named after animals.

A lot it turns out. Oh, so very many!

So, the idea for this field guide, hiking patch quest, and certificate was born.

In the weeks that followed, we scoured over old maps and town histories. We took requests from friends who knew of a rock in their home town that was special. We read books as far reaching as Jan and Christy Butler's *Erratic Wandering* to state geology manuals from the 1950s and 1960s.

And we went out there and found the rocks—not thousands of them, not even hundreds. But we narrowed down a list of twenty mandatory rocks and five optional rocks out of sixteen for you to visit. Visit twenty-five, fill out a form, and you qualify for a patch and certificate.

Remember, our list barely scratches the rock surface in terms of what's out there, and admittedly, the list more or less simply consists of rocks we like.

But we did have some rules, and now those rules are yours as well.

1. **Visit the state.** The Rocks That Rock list will take you from the ocean to the lakes to the mountains and to the cities. Our goal was not just to have you visit a rock and go home, but check out the area, town, and neighborhood where the rock lives! Get some ice cream. Find a museum. Enjoy a park while you're there.
2. **Nothing man made.** For the most part, this is a list of natural formations. We want you to be someplace in the wild. (To be fair, the list does break this rule twice, but you'll see why.)
3. **Anyone and any family can attain this list.** These are easy or relatively easy locations with generally short hikes or no hike at all. We wanted people of any age or ability to touch these rocks. Some of these destinations may even be wheel chair accessible. That said, the optional list has some very hard hikes on it for the more veteran hikers among you. And as far as we know, the only place you can't bring your family pet is Monadnock State Park.
4. **They are free.** The only thing we want this list to cost you is mileage and snacks. For example, we love America's Stonehenge, but there's a ticket price. There are a couple locations within state parks, so there may be a small cost depending on when you go.
5. **They are all on public land.** The rock destinations had to be someplace we could all go that wasn't private property. No permissions needed. That said, a couple of these locations are near the road or right next to private land, so please be respectful.

That's it! The ambitious among you could tag this list in a couple weeks. But maybe you want to make a day trip out of each one. Up to you. There's no time limit involved.

Uma and I are willing to bet that we missed plenty of cool rocks that we just didn't know about. Tell us about them if you find them. Who knows—perhaps there will be updates to this list as we go.

Here's the most important part—this was fun! Every trip and hike offered us a new adventure, something interesting to learn, a new place to explore.

And remember, this is all, always, in the eye of the beholder. I didn't see a Kitty Rock next to Indian Rock in Windham, but Uma did and so it is. Nessie's Humps in Manchester were my idea. Teenage Mutant Ninja Turtle Rock in Auburn? All Uma. Maybe you'll see something different. Maybe you'll think we're crazy! But it's all good. Pack up your little ones (or big ones), grab some munchies, and hike your own hike. Let them run their hands over the granite, or marble, or quartz, and let them tell you what they see. And then report back to us.

You can join our Facebook page—NH Rocks That Rock 25—and download the rules and patch application sheets. Or just email me at rocksthatrock25@gmail.com and I'll send one your way.

Now, enough talk. Get going and find those Rocks That Rock!

—Uma and Dan Szczesny, May, 2021

DRIVE UPS
(all required)

These are rock locations that you can access by car or a short, flat walk.

Big Bertha
749'

Sanbornton
43° 29' 27" -71° 35' 53"

Access: I-93 south, Sanbornton Rest Stop in between exits 22 and 20. The rest stop is accessible only southbound. Pull to the far left (or south) side of the parking area. Big Bertha and surrounding boulders are about fifteen yards up a short path starting at the end of the sidewalk.

Big Bertha is an unusual rock, mainly due to its location. That said, it's also one of the most accessible boulders on this list; it's only a few feet away from a parking area with nearby bathrooms, snacks, and relative isolation. The perfect combination.

There's even a short Boulder Trail of about a quarter mile, in case stretching your legs on Big Bertha isn't enough.

There used to be a sign at the rest stop inviting travelers to visit the woods behind the visitor center. The sign mentioned that taking the trail would lead you to "natural happenings that put you in touch with the resources around you."

Well, the sign is gone, but you can still hang out at the natural happening that's Big Bertha, one of the largest glacier erratics in the state at about twenty feet.

Rock climbers are very familiar with Big Bertha, and she's featured—along with some other boulders nearby—on climbing sites. On their way to or from work, or heading back after bigger day trips, many climbers will stop at Sanbornton Rest Stop for some candy and a quick scramble up Big Bertha. The boulder is considered a class five climb, needing technical equipment.

We visited on the tail end of a full-day trip, and my daughter was far more interested in the vending machines than exploring the boulder area. Word to the wise for parents—those vending machines are available 24/7. If you're going to stop, you best have some change in the car!

What's Nearby: Well, access to the bathrooms is nice! But you're right on the highway. So, your best bet is the next exit down, exit 20. That will pop you right out onto a commercial strip with fast food and outlets. If you're looking for some history, head west on Route 3 and check out the historic Memorial Arch of Tilton.

Boise Rock
1906'

Franconia Notch State Park
44° 09' 09.9" -71° 40' 41.2"

Access: I-93 north drives straight through Franconia Notch State Park. Boise Rock is accessible only on the northbound highway through the notch. Boise Rock pull off is the exit right after Lafayette Campground. There is plenty of parking right next to the short, paved path that leads down to the rock.

Boise Rock has been embedded in New Hampshire folklore since the early 1800s. While not as dramatic as the Cannon Cliff right across the highway, and not as epic as, say, the Flume just down the road, Boise Rock has a more personal and somewhat gruesome story to tell.

When the giant erratic was deposited in the notch way back when, the glacier carved out the lower half, leaving a significant overhang, a partial cave. A couple million years later, this cave would save the life of Thomas Boise, the rock's namesake.

The story goes that one winter night in the early 1800s, Thomas Boise, a teamster from Woodstock, was traveling through Franconia Notch with his horse and sleigh when a ferocious blizzard struck. In order to survive, Thomas took shelter under the overhanging rock, but as the night wore on, he had to resort to drastic measures to survive. Thomas killed his horse, skinned it and wrapped himself in the hide so that he might stay warm enough to survive the night. His plan worked. The next morning, a search party found him under the great rock, the horse hide frozen stiff. Today, the incident is famous as a courageous story of survival, and the giant boulder was given Boise's name.

One more curious thing about this off-the-beaten-path boulder—if you look closely, you'll see that both moss and lichen call the rock their home, a testament to Boise Rock's peculiar geographic location of moisture and sun that allows both organisms to grow there.

What's Nearby: You are in Franconia Notch—the number of things you can do and see are nearly limitless. Start by walking down toward the highway to get a good long look at the spectacular Cannon Cliff. Then, be sure to bring a state park brochure with you. You can check out the Basin, Profile Ledge, the Flume, or just walk the long, paved path that runs through the park by heading north or south from Boise Rock.

Chicken Farmer Rock Newbury
820' 43° 18' 15.6" -72° 00' 38.5"

Access: Right on the north side of Route 103 about two miles south of Newbury town center, nearest address is 539 NH Rt. 103.

Of all the rocks in New Hampshire, all the great stone profiles, all the epic gravity-defying boulders and grand vista facing cliffs, one rock stands above them all in popularity and fame.

We are, of course, talking about the Chicken Farmer I Still Love You Rock.

This painted, overgrown, weedy outcropping along a busy state route is so well known, Google Maps has it pinned as a Historical Landmark. Even Madison Boulder doesn't get that.

But that's accurate because the Chicken Farmer I Still Love You

Rock is all about history, and that history more or less encompasses what it's like to be from and live in New Hampshire where love stories about chicken farmers are entirely relatable.

In short, local legend tells the tale of a hard-working Chicken Farmer and his wife who lived across the road. So hard working to provide for his family was this farmer, that the wife became upset at him for spending so much time away from the family. She lashed out, but instantly regretted her anger. And realizing how grateful she was for her husband, she painted the rock, Chicken Farmer I Love You, as a love note and apology.

Years later, in what was perhaps the greatest small town government mistake of all time, the message was covered, the town deeming it to be graffiti. Petitions were signed. Angry voices expressed outrage. And overnight, a new sign was painted, only this time the word *still* was added. And so it remains.

New Hampshire writer and storyteller Rebecca Rule said the original message and the update are two parts of the same message. "The original is a story of young love," she said. "The revision is the story of unrequited and enduring love. Two beautiful stories; one rock."

The chicken farmer endures.

What's Nearby: Take care, as the rock is alongside the road. Enough people visit the landmark to have created space for parking and a beaten path around the site, but pay attention to the traffic and the private property around the rock. Otherwise, Lake Sunapee is dead ahead; go sit by the shore and contemplate New Hampshire's greatest love story.

Indian Kitty Rocks   Windham
236'   42° 48' 29.40" -71° 16' 45.60"

Access: It sometimes feels like this part of New Hampshire is in a constant state of expansion. Since this set of rocks is right off the highway in one of the busiest parts of the state, time your visit with traffic in mind. This historic collection of boulders is located on the north side of Enterprise Drive about a quarter mile west of the dead-end traffic circle. The quickest way to get there is Exit 2 off the I-93, head west on Route III, make a left on Enterprise Drive. Indian/ Kitty Rocks is located in a small clearing on the north side of the road, but parking is sketchy. If you don't mind a quick road walk, you can park in the dead-end circle near the tower and walk back. *Note: There are two Indian Rocks on this list. The other is in the Pulpit Rock Conservation Area in Bedford.*

Technically, there are five significantly sized rocks in this jumble, and Uma decided they all needed names.

So, with Indian Rock directly in front of you (that's the one with the plaque) if you go clockwise, you'll encounter Turtle Rock, Cheese

Rock, Pizza Rock, and finally, Kitty Rock. Uma wanted only Kitty Rock to count, but given the long history behind Indian Rock, we compromised and renamed the site Indian Kitty Rocks.

Back in 1933 when the town of Windham affixed a memorial plaque to Indian Rock to commemorate the (probably) Pawtucket Nation using these rocks to grind corn, the area around the site looked wildly different. The construction of nearby I-93, coupled with changes and expansion of Indian Rock Road to Route 111, has left this area nearby devoid of most natural features.

Still, some tranquility can be found by walking the twenty-five feet or so up to the town's oldest landmark from the road. There's a bench and some signage there. Uma enjoyed exploring the quartz and mica veins in the rocks, and the jumble is close enough together that kids can hop from rock to rock.

After a little brushing away of dirt and leaves, we were even able to find the grinding holes at the top of the rock where the Native Americans worked their crops. Uma wanted to be clear about Kitty Rock as well—the smaller boulder to the right of Indian Rock appears to have cat ears on either side, as well as a long face, complete, she said, with whiskers (if you look close enough and squint your eyes just so!).

What's Nearby: In the middle of the dead-end circle, likely where you parked, is a grand stone tower built by Al Letizio, Jr., the CEO of nearby A.J. Letizio Sales and Marketing. The tower was completed in 2017 to mark the 275th anniversary of the town and also to honor the memory of Michael Letizio, an Italian immigrant and laborer who worked in the town in the early twentieth century. The tower is worth checking out, and tours are occasionally available. Letizio is even planning some outdoors kids' events in the circle like Rapunzel. Call the town for more info.

Madison Boulder
565'

Madison
43° 55' 52.19" -71° 10' 4.01"

Access: The Madison Boulder Natural Area State Park is home to the largest known glacier erratic in North America. The park is technically always open for recreation, but it never hurts to call ahead (603-227-8745) just to be sure. The address for the park is 473 Boulder Road, Madison. The best access from north or south is off Route 113 about mid-way between Madison proper to the south and Conway to the north. At the end of Boulder Road, you'll come to a gate and parking area. The boulder is an easy walk in on a well-maintained road/trail of about a quarter mile from there.

My daughter was running. At first, I assumed she was charging toward to enormous boulder looming before us, a gigantic, all-encompassing erratic that nearly blocked out the afternoon sun. Not so.

She skidded to a halt alongside the boulder and pointed. "Daddy, look!"

There, about three feet above her head and moving fast was a large, spiky, black caterpillar. How she saw it from a distance was beyond me, but now that we were up close, the Giant Leopard Caterpillar was impossible to miss. He was quickly making his way down the Madison Boulder toward my daughter.

"Can I touch him?"

I shook my head. Those little spikes can be deceiving. "Best we just watch, ok?" I said.

And so we did, my daughter and I. There in the shadow of the largest glacial erratic in North America—a towering 5,000-ton, nearly 100-foot-long monster of a rock—we sat on the grass and watched a caterpillar crawl and I couldn't imagine an any more perfect day.

The boulder has been part of New Hampshire lore since Charles Hitchcock's 1878 geological survey. At one point, there were stairs pounded into the rock to give tourists access to the top. Supposedly, those names are still carved high above our heads. Today, visitors must settle for a ground view—if anyone can settle for a rock that weighs the equivalent of thirty-six blue whales.

"She made it, Daddy," my daughter said. Our caterpillar successfully reached the bottom of the boulder and inched underneath. My daughter finally stood and tilted her head back, taking in the rock. "Big," she said.

What's Nearby: You're in the White Mountain foothills, so there's plenty of nature and trails nearby, including Silver Lake just south. Want to shop? Conway's outlets are massive. But we suggest, this time, stay put. Bring a picnic and spread out in the shadow of this hunk of granite. Or check out some of the shorter hiking trails in the boulder area. Dip your toes in the creek just up the road. Spend the day chatting with Madison Boulder, that rock can teach you a few things!

Nessie's Humps
308'

Manchester
43° 00' 02.8" -71° 27' 16.1"

Access: Of all the neighborhood parks in Manchester, Oak Park is one of the least known. The park is one block large, about 2.6 acres, and borders four streets: Oak Street to the East, Harrison Street to the South, Maple Street to the West, and Brook Street to the North. Nessie's Humps is a series of three rocks jutting out of the ground on a small rise in the north west corner of the park. Parking is free along any of the four street, but the closest and easiest to Nessie's Humps would be Brook Street.

Oak Park is a curiosity. The land was donated back in the early 1920s and was known as Parker Commons for many years. The houses along Oak Street are all newer because there used to be a city reservoir directly across from the park. It often seems like the city itself forgets the park exists. If you happen upon the park just after the city has cut the lawn, it's a great place to play.

With an x-shaped walkway that extends down from all four corners, playground and exercise equipment, and even a shelter with benches in the center, it's a great place for kids and dogs. The neighborhood came together in 1985 to successfully petition the city to erect a flag pole along Maple Street.

The legend of Nessie's Humps dates back to the area's reservoir days when a nearby resident of Scottish descent swore that there was a strange, enormous creature living in the city reservoir. That pool might be long gone, but the rocks remain as a testament to the odd history of Oak Park.

What's Nearby: Manchester's Elm Street is a few blocks away, filled with coffee shops and restaurants. Just two blocks south you have Wagner (Pretty) Park, a lovely garden park right next to the Currier Museum. As long as you're in Manchester, you might want to drive out to the Cedar Swamp Preserve and track down T-Rex Rock, this guide's cover photo and one of the optional hikes on the list!

Old Man of the Valley
700'

Shelburne
44° 23' 5.4" -71° 1' 25.00"

Access: Finding the Old Man is a bit tricky. The formation is located just off the south side of Route 2 in Shelburne, just short of the Maine border. Drive east about 8.8 miles from the intersection of Routes 16 and 2 in Gorham until you come to a small parking area right before Connor Road. Park there and walk back along route two until you come to the end of the guardrail. Follow a woodland path about 100 feet to the Old Man of the Valley.

Since the Old Man of the Mountain fell in 2003, there have been plenty of rock profiles vying to take his place. Some of them are large cliff profiles—the Watcher in Franconia Notch, Indian Head on Mount Pemigewasset, Admiral Dewy Profile on Artist's Bluff, Martha Washington Profile in Crawford's Purchase. You get the idea. The list goes on.

We selected The Old Man of the Valley for two reasons: the formation looks like a mini Old Man of the Mountain, and it's a fairly easy drive up. (Note: the Old Man of Keene is on the optional list, but requires a longer hike.)

It's worth mentioning that this site is also the location of a fairly sizable geo-cache. For those who haven't tried it, geo-caching is a hobby where you use an app to track down a variety of different sized treasure boxes or jars. Some are easy to find, like this one. Others requires more searching. Having a little toy or sticker treasure at the end of or somewhere on a hike gives some added incentive to the littles to reach their goals. Uma always asks if there are any caches on a hike, and indeed we've found a few. Check out the Geocaching app for more.

What's Nearby: You are about as far north as this list will take you, near Gorham and Berlin, with literally thousands of trails and outdoors destinations around every turn! The kids will love the Gorham Moose sculpture in Gorham Common, while Moose Brook State Park is just up the road.

Ordination Rock
624'

Tamworth
43° 51' 18.10" -71° 16' 47.53"

Access: Finding this famous historic rock with the staircase is easy. Ordination Rock rests about one mile west of Tamworth Center along Route 113. You can park along the road, but better yet, turn into the cemetery drive nearly right across the street. Just be careful of traffic when crossing back to the rock.

About two miles north of Ordination Rock, Hidden Automotive can be found. The car repair shop is run by the direct descendants of the Rev. Samuel Hidden who was ordained atop the rock on September 12, 1792. Many sermons were held up there until the good reverend had his own church to preach out of. Today, his grandsons (many times over) guard Samuel's legacy as one of the town's settlers, first preacher and founder of the Tamworth Social Library.

They're so proud, in fact, that Mike Hidden tells of the time the auto shop decorated an old car to look like Ordination Rock, complete with a cenotaph on the roof, to drive in a Fourth of July Parade.

And then there's the Devil's Handprints!

On our trip to Ordination Rock, we looked mightily for the handprints but couldn't find them. According to the Hidden family, Rev. Sam once gave a sermon so fiery that he was able to drive the devil straight out of Tamworth. On his way out, the Devil left his prints on Ordination Rock.

"Daddy, what's that thing," Little Bean said, pointing to the bright white obelisk atop the rock.

The marble marker was installed in 1862, and has inscriptions on all sides, telling of his service in the Revolutionary War and his graduation from Dartmouth. On the north side, the saying reads, "He came into the Wilderness and left it a Fruitful field."

What's Nearby: First, go pay your respects to the good reverend, he's laid to rest at an old table stone in Ordination Rock Cemetery across the street. Then, check out Tamworth. It's a tiny town with a long history. For example, the Barnstormers Theatre is located in Tamworth and is the oldest professional summer theatre in the United States. It was founded in 1931 by Francis Cleveland, the son of our twenty-second President Grover Cleveland.

The Train/Londonderry Boulder   Londonderry
337'   42° 55' 09.8" -71° 24' 02.9"

Access: We're certain you've driven by The Train many times, as it sits on one of the business roads in one of the most densely populated areas near Boston-Manchester Regional Airport. The rock, usually covered in graffiti, can be found jutting out of the embankment on Rockingham Road/Route 28 in North Londonderry near the intersection of Sanborn Road. If you're heading south from Manchester, turn right on Sanborn Road and park in one of the office parking lots then walk back. But of course, be careful of traffic on this very busy road.

Of all the boulders on our list, the Train may have the richest pedigree as the slab that birthed the career of one of the best-known rock climbers in the world.

"I think I was maybe fourteen, driving back from soccer practice with my mom when I saw just one guy on that boulder," said pro climber Joe Kinder. "I was obsessed with climbing but didn't really have any outlets, and I kept getting in trouble as a kid, so my mom just stopped the car and told me to go say hi."

Young Kinder hit the jackpot that day, as the climber working the rock was none other than Brett Meyers, another pro most associated with developing routes on the Pawtuckaway Boulders.

Kinder already had a mentor at Manchester West High School, a guidance councilor named Gary Hunter, himself an amateur climber who encouraged Kinder to climb. But now, with a friendship with Meyers, Kinder's destiny was set.

"Being from New England, it's not easy to find the most profound places to climb," Kinder told me from Las Vegas where he now lives. "But that rock, in terms of rock quality, texture and accessibility, makes it special. It was like our little playground, a practice place where we could have fun and try new things. That place made me!"

Climb in the shadow of the greats, there on a busy state route in Londonderry.

What's Nearby: After you check out the Train, walk back south toward your car and head east or west on the Londonderry section of the rail trail. We recommend west, as that route will take you through interesting old Londonderry center and then you'll pop out near the airport.

Vessel Rock
1033'
Gilsum

Access: Vessel Rock Road, Gilsum

Vessel Rock is a prominent landmark located on Vessel Rock Road, which was originally named for its resemblance to a vessel under sail. A major earthquake in 1817 altered its shape, but the enormous rock, as large as the house next to it, is still a sight to behold.

But, this is someone's backyard. The owners have been generous in allowing the visitors to see the rock, and in fact the town itself features the rock on its website. So, take a look, but only from afar, please.

The real reason Vessel Rock is on our list is because we actually want you to go to Gilsum. You see, despite all the rocks in the White Mountains, Gilsum is the heart and soul of New Hampshire rocks.

Gilsum is where the annual Rock Swap and Mineral Show takes place each summer. The nationally known event raises money for kid's recreation programs and has been run by volunteers for fifty-five years. Why Gilsum? Because the town was the center for mineral mining back in the '40s and '50s. Inactive mines still dot the area.

Want more? The Bear Den Geological State Park is a wonder of rock ledge trails and glacial pot holes. And downstream from the famous Stone Arch Bridge (which you should also visit, see below) is something called the Deep Hole, a natural gorge formation and swimming hole along the Ashuelot River.

What's Nearby: Everything as it turns out! In particular, stop and visit Gilsum's stone arch, keystone bridge, located right off Route 10, carrying Surry Road over the Ashuelot River. There's a small parking space off Surry and you can scramble right to the river edge to catch a look at the arch. Built in 1862, the Keystone is one of the highest arch bridges in the state with the roadway forty-three feet above the river.

SHORT HIKES
(all required)

These are rock locations that require short, simple hikes to get to.

Balance Rock
2100'

Pillsbury State Park
43° 14' 41.40" -72° 6' 31.60"

Access: Pillsbury State Park is one of the more primitive and lesser-known parks in the state system. The main park access is located at 100 Pillsbury State Park Road in Washington. There's no toll on the access road, but stop first at the park office to pay your fee and pick up maps. Check and call ahead for times and reservations.

After checking in at the office, drive down Pillsbury State Park Road until you come to the parking circle near Mill Pond. You can park between the pond and the playground. Walk north out of the parking lot, past the camping area and past the gate. There you'll see the sign for Balance Rock Trail. Bear left and begin your one-mile hike up the shoulder of Bryant Mountain. You'll first reach a small boulder with fantastic views toward North Pond. Then, 0.1 mile further along is enormous Balance Rock.

About a quarter mile up the trail, Uma began counting newts. The park had just gone through a spell of wet, humid weather and the little Eastern Red Spotted Newts darted this way and that across our trail like tiny, shining streaks. My daughter was beyond delighted. I was as well, because by any measure, the Balance Rock Trail is a true New Hampshire trail—plenty of ups and downs, rooty, elevation gain. Without the newts to distract and amaze her, this would be a more complicated climb.

It also was our last. When we reached Balance Rock, our Rocks That Rock list—the one we spent so many hours creating—would be completed. I was glad our little newty friends were accompanying us.

The trail wound upwards, and my daughter tiptoed through the wet brush like a ballet dancer, keeping her eyes peeled as our trail friends skimmed around us. We counted more than a dozen, but missed many more, the mountain eco-system healthy with life and wet with potential.

Before long we were at the boulder, an enormous egg perched atop another, seemingly ready to roll downhill.

"See if you can move it," I told her.

And there atop a small mountain, surrounded by efts, Uma placed her hands upon the boulder and became the first human to complete this list.

"It won't budge, daddy," she said. "Let's find some more newts."

So we did. And now you can too.

What's Nearby: Pillsbury State Park is lovely and dotted with pocket ponds and swamps with excellent shore access. Take your time exploring. Skip a stone. Sit a spell. Find some newts. But if you must, the tiny, nearby tourist town of Washington can provide a picturesque stroll.

The BOB   Concord
660'   43° 13' 33" -71° 37' 38"

Access: The BOB (Big Old Boulder) rests at the end of a quarter mile spur trail off the West End Farm Trail just about 1.3 miles south of Carter Hill Orchard. The trailhead we took to reach it starts at Carter Hill Orchard which is at 75 Carter Hill Road, Concord. (Note: Please be aware that the orchard is a seasonal business and is generally open only until 5:00 or 6:00 p.m. Call or check their website before planning your hike.)

The West End Farm Trail shows up on most GPS devices, but the spur trail may not. The Concord Conservation Commission puts out a series of great maps (West End Farm Trail is Map #26), but be careful because the BOB is actually much closer if you start from Davis Road, but parking is NOT allowed there and is strictly enforced. Best to start from the orchard.

From Carter Hill Orchard, the West End Farm Trail goes to the right of the equipment barns and thru a set of gates. At the bottom, go to the right of the irrigation pond to the other end where you'll follow the High Trail for a quarter mile until you make another right onto the West End Trail. From there, it's 0.5 miles to the old Davis Road. Go left and follow it for 500 feet. Be careful: There's a trail going to the right, and that's not the West End Farm Trail. You need to go a few hundred feet more. From there it's only another 0.5 miles or so until you get to another sharp left bend in the trail, and there will be a sign for the Erratic Boulder. That's BOB. Hang a right.

During our visit, we moved out of the orchard and around the high grass of the irrigation pond. Little Bean stopped short, held up a hand, and said, "What is that?" We froze, and after a few seconds we heard them, a quiet buzz growing loader, echoing off the tree. The chorus of the spring peepers greeted us, and there were hundreds of them. In fact, we could see them rippling through the water.

"Frogs," I said, "many, many frogs!"

And so it goes. The shrill chirp of those creatures followed us up the path, through the deep woods and up the sharp rise to the BOB, a towering mammoth every bit worthy of its title. We ate, played, climbed, but in the back of our heads, we still heard the hum of those frogs.

The frogs call us back, and we must go.

What's Nearby: Carter Hill Orchard is just lovely. Besides the farm stand, there's a playground and a wooden observation tower that puts you above the trees. And of course, cider. And frogs, so many frogs . . .

Boulder Natural Area
350'

Pawtuckaway State Park
43° 06' 58.2" -71° 10' 43.1"

Access: Selecting just one boulder to visit at Pawtuckaway State Park is like picking one star out of the heavens. But we did decide to narrow our directions down to at least one area. The Boulder Natural Area (or Field) is most easily accessed from Round Pond Road, just off Deerfield Road to the north of the park. Once you turn onto Round Pond Road, you'll see a parking area off to your left. From here down to the pond and boulder area, Round Pond Road is gated and becomes more trail-like. Park, walk past the gate, and head down to the pond which will be about 0.75 miles on your left.

Once you're nearly at the water, you'll see Boulder Trail to your right. This was our route into the main area of boulders and slabs. Round Pond Road is accessible from the primary entrance to the park, Reservation Road, as well, but requires a park fee from that side. Also, when we were there, the road around Round Pond was under a foot of water, so call ahead.

There was a moment on the trail heading down toward the boulder field, when a group of kids, some not much older than Little Bean, passed us by dressed in climbing gear. One girl of perhaps eight was barefoot, white chalk on her hands and feet.

"Daddy," Little Bean said, fascinated, "she was climbing rocks barefoot!"

Pawtuckaway State Park, the 5,500-acre jewel in the New Hampshire park system, is a magnet for rock climbing and bouldering. There are hundreds of places with fantastical names, like Magic Pond, Area-51, Blair Wood, and Split Rock—and each area is filled with a variety of rocks.

In the place we were heading, we'd find the Slab, Overlook, Churchill, Pudding, and Storm, among others. But go to a place of magic, and magic often finds you.

After visiting the boulders and enjoying a lunch surrounded by dragonflies atop a rocky perch, we met a recently retired couple from New York City. They had outfitted an old van and were travelling without plans up the east coast, visiting and hiking state parks along the way. The woman, Jan, was a former biologist. The man, Major, was looking for directions to the boulder field where we had just been.

But Little Bean was not having it.

"Here," she said, "look at this."

She led the curious strangers to a small stream where we had just been, and pointed at a tiny pool of minnows flinting in the gleaming pool.

"Well, whatya know," Jan said. So, the four of us sat in the long shadow of the rocks, watching the fish, talking of adventure. The rocks had been there for thousands of years. They could wait a few minutes more.

What's Nearby: If you go to Pawtuckaway, stay in Pawtuckaway. South Mountain with its popular, active fire tower is not far, while in the other direction, North Mountain's 1,000-foot summit beckons. Or maybe find your own boulder and give it a name.

Buffalo Rock
531'

Bow
43° 6' 0" -71° 30' 38"

Access: Nottingcook Forest is a large forest easement held by Bow Open Spaces which offers a series of crisscrossing and unique trails though the streams and run-offs around Great Meadow Pond. Buffalo Rock can be reached via a parking area at the end of Woodhill Hooksett Road off Pine Street heading west off of Route 3A. Continue down Woodhill Hooksett Road, around a gate. The wide old road could be very wet. We took the road past the Sheridan's Way Trail, over a small culvert area where the stream was coming right over the road, and hooked up with a blue blazed trail on our left that brought us back up to Sheridan's Way. About a quarter mile later, the trail passes by Buffalo Rock on the left, which is signed.

Nottingcook Forest is close to everything, but far from the crowds, popular with local organizations like the Girl Scouts, but little known to the outside hiking community.

If you're looking for a perfect beginning hike to reach one of your first rocks, Buffalo Rock is a perfect choice. Little Bean and I nearly ran down the old, wide road, picking at colorful stones as we went. Near the edge of Great Meadow Pond, we were startled by a great splash near the shore, but we couldn't tell if it was a big toad or a beaver that pranked us.

The forest is filled with wonderous destinations with names like Steer Brook Gorge, Six Acre Swamp, and Duckbill Ledge, but we were focused on our only goal.

The trail to Buffalo Rock was perfectly uneventful, the day blue with a steady breeze keeping the bugs at bay. The hike was everything and nothing, woods and moss on rocks, and letting our fingertips drift lazily in the cool stream.

It was late spring when the shooters were beginning to bloom, but the forest still looked open and inviting.

The massive chunk of boulder called Buffalo Rock earns its name by being thick and bulky, sprawling right along the trail. We climbed atop the rock and feasted on strawberries and parmesan. We saw not a single other soul the whole day.

What's Nearby: You are midway between Concord and Manchester, and that puts you within reach of at least four other rocks on this list. Also, an interesting walk around presents itself right in Hooksett; park near Robie's Country Store and take a hike over the Merrimack River on a foot bridge.

Dog Rock
377'

Candia
43° 2' 19" -71° 22' 2"

Access: Tower Hill Pond in Candia provides the hiker with a nearly four-mile loop hike as well as a variety of side trails and off-shoots to explore. The pond, used and controlled by the Manchester Water Works, is heavily trafficked in all seasons and contains mostly wide, easy trails. The quickest route to Dog Rock is to access the pond via Tower Hill Road. If you are coming from the south, look for gate A39, Fire Road #75, park on the road next to the other cars, and head toward the pond. In about 0.5 miles you'll come to the pond junction with the dam on your left and trail on your right. Go right about 0.25 miles until you come to a clear field on your right. Up at the top of that rise in the field is Dog Rock. (Word of warning: If you attempt Dog Rock in the summer, that field will be knee-high in thorny bush.)

For a quick, easy-to-access hike with some distance and water exploration, there's nothing in and around Manchester like Tower Hill Pond. But Little Bean had some other ideas besides a hike. Given how popular this recreation area is, we decided to bring along our metal detector. It was a good call!

But first Dog Rock, a massive rectangular boulder that looks like a dog head on the trail side. During spring and fall, the field is clear and the boulder easy to see. During the summer it's a bit trickier. Little Bean enjoyed walking up the fallen trees to get to the rock.

Before long we had planted ourselves on a bench lookout next to the water and were digging up dirt as our detector rang again and again. Bottle caps, wire, and chunks of what appeared to be melted aluminum were our prizes.

"Daddy," she said, "do you think we'll find gold?"

Alas, if bottle caps were gold, we would have gone home rich.

What's Nearby: On your way back, or after you do a counter clockwise loop, take some time to explore the rock outcroppings around the dam area. The Northern Water Snake is well known in this area and the non-venomous, popular snake can often be found basking on rocks. If snakes aren't your thing, TMNT Rock is not far from you in nearby Auburn!

Elephant Head Rock
1996'

Crawford Notch State Park
44° 12' 48.6" -71° 24' 22.4"

Access: Elephant Head Rock in Crawford Notch has been appearing on postcards and engravings for 150 years. Historian Ron Walters said there's written mention of the rock formation as far back as 1840, and most likely was called that when the original road was being built through the notch between 1800–1820. Elephant Head Rock is one of the best known and most visited rock cliffs in New Hampshire, if not New England.

In Twin Mountain, at the junction of Routes 3 and 302, head east on Route 302 for about 8.5 miles until you pass the Highland Center. Just beyond that, past Saco Lake on your left and Crawford Depot Station on your right, is a small parking area. Take the Webster-Jackson Trail, across the street from the parking area, for about 0.1 miles where you will see a well-marked side trail on your right to Elephant Head. In about 0.25 miles, you're there. Be aware that the top of Elephant Head Rock is a cliff, so keep the little ones close when you're up there.

This was our first rock on the list, though we didn't know it at the time. Here's what I wrote back when Little Bean was Baby U:

Baby U cups her hands and digs into a thin layer of gravel, rocks, and dirt. The wind at the top of Elephant Rock in Crawford Notch comes up the valley and tussles her already wild and unruly wall of hair. We've been exploring the AMC's Highland Center area of the notch these past couple days, just her and I—dipping our feet into the muddy water, picking wild flowers in the fields near the center, crawling and climbing on any stable surface, and a few unstable ones.

We are exhausted, and filthy, and we both stink.

But our eyes are clear, and she looks up at me with a handful of dirt and twigs and roars like a tiny twenty-five-pound dinosaur and dumps the entire concoction into my own outstretched hand.

Little woods hikes like these give her a first look at the wild world, and they train me how to walk with her on my back. So, we hike, little by little, inch by inch. First, a round trip of about 0.75 miles up to this extraordinary lookout shaped like the head of an elephant, about 600 feet above the notch that marks the entrance to Crawford Notch.

And besides singing "The Wheels on the Bus Go Round and Round" about 1,000 times, Baby U is perfectly at home on my back, patting the back of my head saying "hat, hat" over and over at my bandana.

She is still fearless. Steep cliffs, buzzing bees, mushrooms—none of those things appear to give her any pause at all, and we'll have to work on that some. But for now, we have this little summit to ourselves with no worries.

She goes back for another load of rocks, stumbles, and goes down in the dirt. I move to sweep her up, but instead she just wipes her hands on her sweater and moves on. She's focused, happy, disheveled, in the mountains.

And dirty. But the dirt just makes us stronger.

What's Nearby: So much! First, knock another rock location off your list by visiting the Highland Center's Playscape. It's possible once your little ones are there, that'll be it for the rest of your visit. They may not want to leave. If it's cool, perhaps the Highland Center has a fire going? Maybe there's some fly fishermen casting in the lake? If you're lucky a tourist train will motor by. Or just find a bench and relax in the wild flowers.

Frog Rock

714'

New Boston

42° 55' 56.54" -71° 43' 23.55"

Access: The rock that started it all. From Route 13 heading north through Mont Vernon, go left on Francestown Turnpike, also known as 2nd New Hampshire Turnpike. Drive about three miles. The southern entrance to Frog Rock Road (now an abandoned access road) will be on your right, just after a long left turn with warning sign arrows. If you reach Hopkins Road, you've gone too far. Parking is available at the side of the road for perhaps two cars.

The dirt road path will reach some stone barriers at about 0.1 miles and a sign indicating that you are entering Frances Hildreth Townes Memorial Forest. Continue down the trail road for about 0.35 or so until you see a clear side path on your right. Take that fifty-feet or so to Frog Rock.

It was Frog Rock that started it all. The list. The patch. The book you hold. Somewhere along the way, Little Bean wanted to find more rocks shaped like creatures. And once that door opened, there was no closing it.

And perhaps unlike many of the other rocks on this list, there's very little debate over Frog Rock's namesake. From a particular angle, the ten-foot erratic looks exactly like what it's named after. So much so, in fact, that Frog Rock used to be a popular destination in the days of the grand hotels.

There were five grand (and grand-ish) hotels in the Mont Vernon area around the mid- to late nineteenth century that drew tourists from the south as far away as Boston. The ladies and children would summer at the resorts while the men would work and come up on the weekends. That meant the hotels would need to keep their guests occupied, and one way to do that was to plan picnic excursions into the countryside. One of those resorts, the Grand Hotel, would send wagonloads of guests to visit what their literature called Bull Frog Rock.

Today, the pasture land that once made up the area has been reclaimed by the forest, but through it all, Frog Rock reigns supreme.

What's Nearby: You're close enough to Monkey Rock to do a drive by, and if you like painted rocks, New Boston residents are proud of their Sunday Driver Rock, a painted message rock alongside Bedford Road just east of town center.

Indian Rock
360'

Bedford
42° 56' 41.80" -71° 35' 58.10"

Access: Indian Rock is just one feature in the small but remarkable Pulpit Rock Conservation Area in Bedford. To reach the Gage's Mill Trailhead, turn onto Pulpit Road from New Boston Road and drive 0.72 miles. The parking area is on your right, just after 144 Pulpit Road.

The trail to Indian Rock is only about a mile round trip and is a wide, crushed gravel path the entire way. Head down from the trail head on Gage's Mill Trail. After about 0.25 miles you'll go right at a sign pointing to Indian Rock, that's Pulpit Brook Trail. Soon you'll see a path to the right that takes you over a bridge and up a short bump to Indian Rock.

On the other side of the park, the rocky gorge called the Pulpit was formed about 14,000 years ago by glacial runoff. The plunge basin and significant ledge resembles a church pulpit, now called Pulpit Rock. At one time, the Pulpit area was a privately owned tourist attraction with a carriage road bringing visitors for sightseeing. Picnics and dancing took placed at a pavilion near the Pulpit, while preachers would stand up top and try to convert the partying flock below. A staircase and boardwalks allowed visitors to inspect the top of the Pulpit, but the hurricane of 1938 made quick work of that.

The Pulpit still exists, of course, along with the ruins of Gage's Mill. But our (and your) destination is special—a single round erratic up on its own little rise amid the birch and poplar.

Little Bean charged up the hill and bee-lined for the little crawl space on the south side of the rock, under an overhang.

"Daddy, you can get inside!" she said. It's a tight squeeze for an adult, but for a little rock hopper, it's perfect. The legend of the rock is that it was used as a stone seat, a favorite place for Native American medicine men to fast.

Indian Rock shouldn't be any more special than any number of fifteen-foot boulders, but there's something about the surrounding knoll and quiet forest—a connection to the past perhaps. The boulder has energy. Give it a listen.

What's Nearby: The park itself with its pulpit and gorge is worth exploring, with several erratics here and there. Off the Tufts Trail, you can visit Hippo Rock, and another unnamed boulder about the same size as Indian Rock can be found near the junction of the Ravine Trail. Perhaps someone should visit and name it?

Sheep (Dog) Rock
306'

Hooksett
43° 6' 1" -71° 26' 19"

Access: Head's Pond Trail in Hooksett is a straight, flat, wide and easy in and out that leads past Heads Pond and back. Coming from the south, parking for the rail trail can be found on Route 3/28 just north of Post Road. Park in the lot, then walk north down to the rail trail. Turn right and hike about 0.7 miles until you come to a clear side path that leads out to the pond. Sheep Rock is about 100 feet down this path on the left.

There is some hub-bub, as there always is in small towns, about what exactly this boulder resembles. Some longtime Hooksett residents insist the rock resembles a hangdog. Some see a gorilla. But there was no question in Little Bean's mind as she climbed the rock's southern face.

"It's a sheep," she said, and since she's the boss, that rock is hereby a sheep.

This section of the Hooksett Rail Trail is a thing of wonder. Long, even, flat and designed for animal lovers, families and most levels of accessibility, the trail still finds a way to feel natural and woodsy. Even when it passes behind apartment complexes, the trail never loses its back-woods feel.

We saw a crane out on the pond, and watched a couple young fishermen pull sunfish from the cold water. Right near the side trail, a stump, half gnawed by a beaver, provides an excellent platform for pictures.

On the way back, we stopped to eat lunch atop a long flat boulder only a tenth of a mile from the parking lot. And as we sat atop the stone, Uma ran her hand across its gritty surface and proclaimed, "This is whale rock."

Thar she blows!

What's Nearby: Continue east on the path where it ends at a pretty section of Head's Pond. There by the water you'll find yet another interesting stone covered in delightful graffiti.

TMNT Rock Auburn
531' 42° 59' 25" -71° 20' 14"

Access: Teenage Mutant Ninja Turtle Rock is a small, sometimes covered, waist-high boulder near the summit of little Mine Hill in Auburn. A section of the rock looks just like one of the cartoon ninja fighters. The trailhead and parking area are on Rt. 121, just about a mile south of the junction with Hooksett Road in the center of Auburn. Park at a pull-off at the shore of Lake Massabesic, immediately north of Shore Road. On the opposite side of the road, look for the sign Gate A21, Fire Road #42. That's your trail!

Head up the fire road until you come to a large open field in about 100 yards. Stay to the right as the trail heads up into the woods. Continue up for about 0.4 miles, always keeping to the right, until you see a dilapidated set of steps built into the ground.

These are the old steps that led up the fire tower that used to be at the summit. The foundations of the tower and debris are still there. Climb to the top of the steps and make a right, keeping the No Trespassing signs to your left. At about the 0.5-mile mark, look right into the woods and you'll see TMNT Rock about ten feet in.

This trail was the one Little Bean asked to come back to. Asked to bring her momma along. Asked if we could visit the rock again, to show off her find. This rock is all hers.

Our original intent was to climb the hill to find the tower, Little Bean being a fire tower buff. But the hike became more. We found a family of tiny mice, entrenched in their rotten log home. We found a dead porcupine and took home some quills which Little Bean used to paint a portrait of that creature, creating a permanent record. And we imagined what it must have been like to be up in that tower, looking over the great Massabesic.

Certain trails leave a mark. Mine Hill is ours.

What's Nearby: After your hike, cross back to your car and spend some time exploring the lake. At times of low water, the shore can be full of clams and crabs. If you have a little more time, visit the Massabesic Audubon Center. And if you're so inclined, stop in the lot near the Massabesic traffic circle and watch the sailboats drift by.

OPTIONAL HIKES/DRIVE UPS
(pick five)

Whether you wish to complete your quest on drive-ups, easy walks, or difficult hikes, this final list has them all. Pick five of the following sixteen and finish your quest!

Big Rock Caves (Mt Mexico)
43° 55' 36.30" -71° 19' 18.00"

Access: Mount Mexico is a low, 2,000-foot summit in the White Mountain Sandwich Range. The trailhead to Big Rock Cave, a unique, above-ground set of slab boulders that form a dynamic shelter cave, begins in Wonalancet on Route 113A. From Chocorua, at the junction of Route 16, drive west on Route 113 for about three miles into Tamworth. Make a right onto Route 133a and drive about 6.3 miles until you see the trailhead parking area on your right. The trail to the cave—Cabin Trail to Big Rock Cave Trail—is about 3.4 miles up and back.

The Big Rock Cave Trail is used by hikers primarily to reach the summit of Mount Paugus, which is on the 52 With a View hiking list. But the Big Rock Cave is an excellent destination in and of itself. Once you cross over the unmarked Mount Mexico, you'll begin to descend and soon come across a handful of free-standing boulders. Just beyond them, the Big Rock Cave is unmistakable. You can, in fact, walk fully from one side of the cave to the other.

What's Nearby: If you feel ambitious, you're about half way to Mount Paugus, a tough little mountain currently sitting on the 52 With a View quest list. Our recommendation: Stay put, bring a picnic and lay out next to pretty Whiting Brook in the shadow of the Big Cave!

Photo of a hiker in front of Big Cave Rocks, courtesy of Cheryl Kreinbring.

Eunice "Goody" Cole Memorial Stone (Hampton)
42° 56' 00.2" -70° 50' 05.3"

Access: The stone sits in directly in front of the Tuck Museum of Hampton History at 40 Park Avenue, directly across from Founders Park.

The stone is a memorial, erected in 1963, to commemorate the only women convicted of witchcraft in the state's history. Eunice Cole has a long and terrible history with New Hampshire, being accused of witchcraft three times, starting in 1656. She was never executed, but she spent time in prison before dying around 1680. Eunice's story is interesting enough to warrant a visit, but right next to her stone can be found Thorvald Rock, supposedly marking the AD 1004 grave of Thorvald, brother of Viking explorer Leif Eriksson and son of Erik the Red. And right down the street can be found Bound Rock, on Woodstock Street. This curious well-like structure marks the start of a boundary line between Hampton & Salisbury created in 1657.

What's Nearby: You can make a whole trip out of all the historic rocks and stones to be found in this area, but remember you're also right next to the ocean, so go collect some seashells as well!

Gilfillan Rock (Concord)
43° 12' 33.0" -71° 35' 52.0"

Access: This historic rock ledge can be found near the summit of Jerry Hill inside the fairly new Marjorie Swope Park in Concord. Primary access to the trail up to the rock can be found on Long Pond Road. Our total loop from the parking area, up to Gillfillan Rock, past the foundation of the old observation tower and back to where we started, was about 1.65 miles.

When John Swope entrusted the seventy-seven-acre Marjorie Swope Park to Concord in 2012, he was basically giving nature lovers the backyard he had shared with his wife for years. Named after Marjorie, a long-time member of the City Council who also served as the chair of the Concord Conservation Commission, the park is a lovely gem just west of downtown.

The Gillfillan Rock, however, has been a prominent feature of the area since long before John and Marjorie. The named carved into the south facing side of the rock dates to 1893, the year that nearby St. Paul's School student Joseph Gilfillan passed away unexpectedly. Since then, the spot has been a popular gathering spot for generations of students, and many names and initials are carved into the top of the rock. Can you read any of them?

What's Nearby: Be sure to continue west from the rock for fifty feet to check out a wonderful view spot and bench. And don't forget, the BOB is also located in Concord, but tagging both in one day would require strict planning and lots of snacks!

Glen Boulder (Pinkham Notch)
44° 14' 17" -71° 16' 26" (3,717 feet)

Access: At 3,717 feet, Glen Boulder is the highest rock on our list and also the most difficult, serious hike. The Glen Boulder Trail can be reached on the west side of NH Route 16 at the Glen Ellis Falls parking lot. From there, it's about 1.6 miles to the boulder of rather rough climbing with an elevation gain of about 1,750 feet, but it does reach tree line quickly.

Glen Boulder is legendary; perhaps not as much at Madison Boulder, but close. Named for the nearby settlement of Glen (the Gaelic word describing a mountain alley) the boulder looks like it's perilously balancing on a steep slope. But don't worry, you can't push it off!
    The area around the boulder is open tundra which gives the hiker amazing views in all directions. But because you are above tree line, please be aware of inclement weather.
    Fun fact—Glen Boulder is not technically a glacial erratic due to the fact that it's made of the same rock that it rests upon.

What's Nearby: If you're not too exhausted after this hike, head on up to the Highland Center area in Crawford Notch and tag the Playscape Playground and Elephant Head to click off three rocks on your list!

Photo of Carter DeMartin, six, courtesy of Jill Kropp

Goodrich Rock (Waterville Valley)
43° 59' 14" -71° 30' 34"

Access: Goodrich Rock is an enormous boulder that you can climb via ladder. Parking and trailhead are off West Branch Road. From Exit 28 on I-93, drive about ten miles northeast and turn left onto Tripoli Road. In 1.2 miles, bear right and continue 0.6 miles down Tripoli Road. Turn right onto West Branch Road and immediately bear left into the parking area.

Though not as grand as the Boulder Field in Pawtuckaway, the hike out to Goodrich Rock does offer some lovely rock hopping, and one area where you walk straight through a split boulder. And while the four-mile hike is not short, the elevation gain from trailhead to the rock is only about 700 feet.

Also, it's not just one path. From the parking area you'll hike from Livermore Road to the Greeley Ponds Trail to the Goodrich Rock Trail. But once atop that boulder, sweeping views await you across the valley toward Sandwich Dome.

What's Nearby: Besides dozens of skiing and hiking trails, the main section of Waterville Valley offers shopping and cafes. But our favorite is the Rey Cultural Center and the Curious George Cottage. Margret and H.A. Rey, authors of the Curious George children's book series, were former summer residents of Waterville Valley and you can visit their renovated cottage, now a cultural learning center.

Photo courtesy of David Kiley and WM Moose

Humongous Boulder, Stoddard Rocks (Stoddard)
43° 7' 16.10" -72° 3' 50.20"

Access: Very limited parking to the trailhead is on Shedd Hill Road. A bit more parking might be found further north at Highland Lake Marina at 1219 Shedd Hill Road.

Let's be honest—they aren't easy to get to, and it's a long hike, about a five-mile round trip up to about 1,600 feet. Plus, the Stoddard Conservation Commission that helps manage the 730-acre property, offers a—how shall we put this—less than user-friendly map.

But, make it up to the top of that hill and wonders await in the form of an entire mountaintop covered with extraordinarily large boulders. We've decided to focus on just one—literally named Humungous Boulder. All told, there are about a dozen enormous boulders, all named, and a loop trail over the summit area of about 0.3 miles to take you around the area. Humungous Boulder is near the back of the summit area, a stand-alone thirty-footer living up to its name.

What's Nearby: Honestly, Stoddard Rocks will likely take up most of your day. But you're pretty close to Pitcher Mountain Fire Tower which has a splendid blueberry bush field in the early summer. And Highland Lake is certainly worth a look!

Photo courtesy of David Kiley and WM Moose

Monkey Rock (New Boston)
42° 59' 34.4" -71° 43' 57.0"

Access: South side of Route 136 (Francestown Road) about three miles north of New Boston town center heading toward Francestown.

Back when New Hampshire storyteller Fritz Weatherbee was wearing white tennis shorts and producing a travel show called Just Up the Road, he made a pitstop along the road to Francestown where he became memorably excited about visiting Monkey Rock.

Rightfully so. Little Bean shared his excitement upon seeing the giant head poking out of the embankment, and we decided to include this odd feature in our list.

Be careful, though, as this is a state road and there is no dedicated parking to visit Monkey Rock. You'll have to find a spot along the road. Watch for traffic!

What's Nearby: Monkey Rock is only about seven miles from the trailhead that leads to Frog Rock. If you get one, you ought to get both!

Old Man of Keene (Keene)
42° 57' 34.0" -72° 15' 45.5"

Access: Beaver Brook Falls Natural Area is a lightly used nature walk, partially along an abandoned road just north of downtown Keene. Trailhead and parking area are at the end of Washington Street Extension. To get there, take Washington Street south from Rt. 9, turn left onto Old Concord Road, then immediately take another left onto Washington Street Extension. Drive to the end and park near the gate

Boy, does New Hampshire miss the Old Man of the Mountain. Luckily, there are plenty of profiles within reach of the casual walker, like this little surprise along the "trail" to Beaver Brook Falls.

The trail itself is an abandoned road, presumably after Washington Street proper was built. From the parking area, take the road trail about 0.8 miles to the top of the waterfall. You can follow a beat path down to the pool. Then, on your way back, you see the Old Man of Keene jutting out into the road. Be sure to pat his nose if you can reach!

What's Nearby: Downtown Keene is right down the road and filled with plenty of shops and other sites. And two other lovely parks with trails—Robin Hood Park and Drummer Hill Conservation Area—are nearby.

Papoose Rock (Lyme)
43° 46' 54.50" -72° 6' 21.50"

Access: Papoose Rock is located near Holt's Ledge along the Papoose Ski Trail at Dartmouth Skiway, where you'll park at 39 Grafton Turnpike Road, Lyme Center.

For this hike, you'll be following the AT south for a rigorous hike up to Holt's Ledge, then back down along the Papoose Ski Trail. All told, this is about a 2.5- mile loop.

Papoose Rock, which can be found about 0.2 miles down the Papoose Ski Trail, stands out on the right side. The twenty-foot erratic features a large overhanging cap as its top layer. We were unable to find any history on why the rock (or ski trail) is called Papoose.

What's Nearby: Of note, along the wide-view precipitous cliffs of Holt Ledges is fencing which is designed not only to protect hikers, but also to keep safe the peregrine falcons who nest on the cliff. Before being protected by the Endangered Species Act, peregrines were driven out of New England by the ravages of DDT. Holt's Ledge was one of the first sites in New Hampshire where peregrines were successfully reintroduced. If you see any, take plenty of pictures, but be sure to leave them be!

Photo from the author's collection

Playscape Playground (Highland Center, Pinkham Notch)
44° 13' 09.0" -71° 24' 46.7"

Access: The Appalachian Mountain Club's Highland Center is located in Crawford Notch along Route 302 nearly across from Saco Lake. Park right in the Highland Center lot.

While the huge Playscape Playground behind the Highland Center breaks pretty much every rule to get onto this list—it's man-made for example—there really was no question in our minds that this is a perfect rocky destination.

Built in 2013 and designed to mimic the natural formations and features a hiker might find along the White Mountain trails, the Playscape features granite boulders, logs and rope bridges, rock walls to free climb, a cave and a tree in the center. There's even a sandbox for very little ones. We felt the uniqueness of the Playscape, coupled with this beautiful area, made it a destination in and of itself!

What's Nearby: We suggest coupling any trip to the Playscape with a hike up Elephant Head Rock, which is right across the street. Want more? Check out Saco Lake or the nearby wildflower field.

Photo by Dennis Welsh, courtesy of AMC

Quimby's Pillow (Mount Moriah, Gorham)
44° 20' 43.6" -71° 08' 34.6"

Access: This unique and little-known boulder is located about 3.5 miles up the Carter-Moriah Trail on the way up to Mount Moriah. The trailhead and parking are located at the end of Banger Road in Gorham. From Gorham, follow Route 2 east from about a half mile from its junction with Route 16, then turn sharply onto Banger Street and drive to the end.

We didn't say they'd all be easy! The boulder sits at about 3,400 feet up the trail, which means your elevation gain is about 2,600. And you won't get any views unless you continue on to tag Mount Moriah.

But we felt that it was important to tell Professor E.T. Quimby's story, which we first learned about atop Mount Kearsarge where his name is carved into stone with a date: 1872. In the mid-1800s, the government was working on mapping New Hampshire and the White Mountains, so they hired Dartmouth geology professor Quimby to get the job done. He and his colleagues used triangulation to map the Whites, and one of the peaks he occupied in 1879 was Mount Moriah. Thus, Quimby's Pillow was named after the good professor!

What's Nearby: First, if you made it that far, you're only three quarters of a mile from the summit. Give it a shot if you and your little one aren't too tired. Views are lovely from up there. Second, as long as you're in Gorham, continue east on Route 2 to tag another rock on the list, the Old Man of the Valley.

Photo courtesy of Steve Smith

Sarcophagus (Mount Monadnock)
42° 51' 47.3" -72° 05' 52.0"

Access: The Sarcophagus can be found on Mount Monadnock. This large, flat glacial erratic landmark is located on the Pumpelly Trail, just above the junction with the Spellman Trail. There are a couple routes to get to it, but the Pumpelly is the most direct (though long)—about 3.7 miles from East Lake Road in Dublin Village.

No rock destination list would be complete without some reason to head to Monadnock State Park. But Monadnock can be tricky. First, there's an entrance fee if you come in from the visitor center side. You can avoid that by hiking up via the Pumpelly. Keep in mind: as best we can tell, Sarcophagus is the only rock on the list unavailable to dogs, as they aren't allowed in the park.

Besides the summit, there are quite a few other rocks and destinations in and around the park—the Tooth, Monte Rosa, Bald Rock, to name a few. Thoreau's Seat is our favorite. The great Transcendentalist visited the mountain at least four times and encouraged visitors to view Monadnock before stepping foot on it. He wrote, "Those who climb to the peak of Monadnock have seen but little of the mountain. I came not to look *off from* it, but to look *at* it. The view of the pinnacle itself from the plateau below surpasses any view which you get from the summit."

What's Nearby: We agree with Henry David. Take some time in the park itself. Stop at the visitor center. Find the views. One bit of advice: if you do decide to tackle the Spellman Trail to the Sarcophagus, take it up, not down. It's quite steep!

Photo courtesy of Christopher DiLoreto

Tippin' Rock (Swanzy)
42° 49' 25.93" -72° 17' 14.15"

Access: The trailhead that leads up Hewes Hill and the Tippin Rock can be found in a hayfield on Warmac Road. The small parking area is nearly directly across from Chebaco Kennel at 95 Warmac Road. The trail to the rock from the field is only about half a mile and gains about 300 feet.

Tippin Rock has been a hiking destination for more than a century! Today, the land is preserved under the Monadnock Conservancy and is a real underused area; few hikes offer such views for so little effort. The outlooks further up from the rock are also popular among bird watchers during spring and fall migrations.

The key to visiting Tippin Rock is, of course, to challenge the legend that with a shove of your shoulder under the right spot you can make forty tons of granite rock gently, like a baby's cradle. Good luck and let us know if you had any more success than us. Either way, unpack your lunch and enjoy some time in the rock's shade, like decades of hikers before you!

What's Nearby: You're not far from Keene. And that means you're not far from the Old Man of Keene rock profile. Two rocks in one day is always a great get!

Photo courtesy of David Kiley and WM Moose

T-Rex Rock (Manchester)
43° 02' 31.0" -71° 29' 42.0"

Access: This enormous trailside rock resembling a T-Rex head rests inside Cedar Swamp Preserve in Manchester. This little known, but wonderful 640-acre preserve is the largest conservation area in the city and contains about two miles of well-maintained trails and some of the oldest black gum trees in the state. The trailhead is located on Countryside Boulevard in the Hackett Hill section of Manchester's Northwest side about a half mile south of Hackett Hill Road.

Clocking in at just under two miles for the complete loop around the preserve, T-Rex Rock is still tricky to find because the dino head faces away from the trail! And there's lots to do and see along the way.

About 100 feet into the path, The Woodland Trail breaks left and right into its loop. But right at that junction is a fantastic scattering of rocks and boulders to enjoy. Continue counter clockwise on the Woodland Path, past the swamp lookout (there's a sign) and up a small rise until you see a jumble of boulders to your left. This is about a half mile from the junction. Go off trail on a beat path and walk down behind the biggest boulder, turn around and there he is, T-Rex Rock!

What's Nearby: As of this writing, a new all-access trail is being constructed through the preserve called the All-Persons Trail, so that should open up the preserve to much more traffic. And of course, while you're in Manchester, don't forget to stop by Nessie's Humps in Oak Park!

Underhill's Chair (Isle of Shoals)
42° 58' 23.3" -70° 36' 50.7"

Access: At the far southern point of Star Island among the Isle of Shoals is a jumble of rocks with one slab, like a table cliff, that juts out over the ocean. This is the infamous Underhill's Chair. Several tour operators run boats and ferries out to the island, including Island Cruises out of Rye and Isle of Shoals Steamship Company out of Portsmouth.

The legend of thirty-four-year-old teacher Miss Nancy Underhill and her tragic demise at the hands of a rogue wave that washed her out to the ocean from this prominent outcrop dates to 1848. And for the most part, the legend appears to be true!

Underhill was a Methodist minister and teacher born in Chester and was working in Portsmouth while travelling back and forth to the island sewing bedding. Nancy would often visit that outcrop to contemplate the "sublime works of God," one reporter wrote. But it wasn't a rogue wave, apparently. Alas, companions said that Nancy crawled down the rock near the water, and when the tide rolled in, she was, according one breathless writer, "launched into eternity."

Launched into eternity. What a way to go.

What's Nearby: The tour companies offer a full range of guided and self-guided tours, and they will also just take you out there and drop you off. One assured us that an hour was more than enough time to get there, find the rock and make it back. We suggest making a day or at least an afternoon of it to give yourself enough time to enjoy this unique place. But please, watch the tides!

Photo: "Miss Underhill's Chair," by Davis Bros. Portsmouth NH, 1870

Wolf Rock (Mason)
42° 44' 56.87" -71° 45' 34.29"

Access: Take Route 123 to Mason town center, then make a left on Meeting House Road northeast for 0.3 miles. On your right is a scrubby parking area in front of Scripts Lane. Hike down unmaintained Scripts Lane for about 0.4 miles until you come to the second prominent path on your left. About fifty feet down that path is Wolf Rock, with the name prominently engraved into it.

The legend of Wolf Rock makes this an easy choice for inclusion on our list. In November of 1757, prominent preacher and early settler Rev. Francis Worcester was approached by six snarling, hungry wolves on his way home.

The reverend scrambled up to the top of the nearest boulder and spent the night swatting back the frenzied wolves with his cane, calling for help. One version of the survival story tells of the ingenious preacher sprinkling down loose tobacco on the wolves, sending them into coughing and sneezing fits.

The next morning, a passerby found the reverend in a state of cold disarray there atop the rock and helped him home where he recovered with a breakfast hot toddy and porridge. In the years since, many have come to pay their respects to the preacher's survival story, and somewhere along the way, "Wolf Rock" was emblazoned with its name.

What's Nearby: If you continue past Wolf Rock, you'll come to the Boston and Maine Rail Trail. Back in town is the boyhood home of Sam Wilson, the meat-supplier who is said to have inspired the Uncle Sam character. And nearby is Pickity Place, a cottage thought to be the inspiration for the grandmother's house in "Little Red Riding Hood."

Photo: Wolf Rock in 1909, Mason, New Hampshire; from an old postcard

Bibliography

AMC White Mountain Guide, edited and compiled by Steve Smith. Appalachian Mountain Club Books, 30th edition, 2017.

Butler, Jane and Christy. *Erratic Wanderings: An Explorer's Hiking Guide to Astonishing Boulders in Maine, New Hampshire and Vermont.* U.S.A. Self-published, 2018.

Eusden, J. Dykstra, Davis, P. Thom, Boisvert, Richard and four others. *The Geology of New Hampshire's White Mountains.* Durand Press, 2013.

Freedman, Jacob. *The Geology of the Mount Pawtuckaway Quadrangle.* New Hampshire State Planning and Development Commission, 1950.

Julyan, Robert and Mary. *Place Names of the White Mountains.* University Press of New England, 1993.

MacGray, Ken. *New Hampshire's 52 With a View: A Hiker's Guide.* U.S.A. Self-published, 2020.

Myers, T.R. and Stewart, Glenn. *The Geology of New Hampshire.* New Hampshire State Planning and Development Commission, 1956.

Acknowledgments

Inevitably, questions will arise about how a six-year-old is able to write a book.

Well, Little Bean did not, of course, do the actual writing. That was done by her co-author. But Uma was involved in every step of this project—selecting the sites, visiting them, grading them on an accessibility scale, suggesting routes. Everything was run by her, all the stories were approved by both her and myself, and of course, she designed the patch and we co-designed the certificate that will accompany this field guide.

And so, I begin by thanking my guiding light, Little Bean, whose unwavering enthusiasm and humor made and continues to make it all worth it.

Developing a project of this scope and detail with a six-year-old requires a support team, and that's exactly what we had—from the moment we began jotting down possible rock locations and plotting out our times and routes to find the rocks.

The long list of individuals we'd like to thank for their enthusiasm, advice, suggestions, wayfinding and general support include, but are not limited to: Ken Bennett, Jane Byam, Ken, Paula and Erin Cayer, Bill Chatfield, John Clayton, Bob Cottrell, Stephen Crossman, Christopher DiLoreto, Linda Feinberg, David and Aislinn Graves, Carrie Ann Gray, Mike Hidden, Gary Hunter, Joe Kinder, Cheryl Kreinbring, Jill Kropp and Carter DeMartin, Matt Landry, Al Letizio, Jr., Virginia Lupi, Ken MacGray, Cassandra Mason, Pricilla Merrill, David Kiley and WM Moose, Christopher Morris, David Morrison, Rebecca Rule, Eric Schwartz, Steve Smith, Don Soule, Ron Walters, Chris Whiton and Zoe Wroten-Heinzmann.

Uma would like to thank Uncle Bob Mackenzie for taking her to Lake Sunapee, one of her favorite places on the planet, and for giving daddy time to write. She would also like to thank Noodles the Newt and his dozens of brothers and sisters who brought us so much joy in Pillsbury State Park.

To the poet Ed Pacht for being our laureate of the rocks.

To our family who continues to come along on this ride no matter how crazy, time consuming and all-encompassing each new project ends up being. Thank you, Andrea, John, Ben, Max, Kiran, Rita, Sandeep and Candace. Thanks, Mom. Thanks, Dad.

To Kirsty Walker and my publisher Hobblebush Books who just lets us write and makes the whole thing better.

And from Uma and Dan to our mom and wife, Meenakshi, who truly is the rock of our family and who is the strongest person we know—and she needs to be in order to put up with our shenanigans. Thank you and we love you!

Elephant Head Rock, photo courtesy of Chris Whiton

About the Authors

Dan Szczesny is a long-time writer, journalist and speaker living in New Hampshire with his daughter and wife.

Uma Szczesny is a long-time playground aficionado and consumer of pizza, cucumbers, and ice cream. She is also one of the youngest hikers to earn her New Hampshire State Fire Tower Quest Patch at the age of four and a half, and the first person to earn a New Hampshire Rocks That Rock 25 Quest Patch. If Uma had her way, she'd do nothing but play Realm Craft on her computer all day.

The two are currently working on playing a game of tag in every state park in New Hampshire. For more on their work and Dan's books, visit danszczesny.com.

NH Rocks That Rock 25

Drive Ups (all required)
These are rock locations that you can access by car or a short, flat walk.

	Comments
Big Bertha (*Sanbornton*) Date: _____	
Boise Rock (*Franconia Notch*) Date: _____	
Chicken Farmer Rock (*Newbury*) Date: _____	
Indian Kitty Rocks (*Windham*) Date: _____	
Madison Boulder (*Madison*) Date: _____	
Nessie's Humps (*Manchester*) Date: _____	
Old Man of the Valley (*Shelburne*) Date: _____	
Ordination Rock (*Tamworth*) Date: _____	
The Train (*Londonderry*) Date: _____	
Vessel Rock (*Gilsum*) Date: _____	

Short Hikes (all required)
These are rock locations that require short, simple hikes to get to.

	Comments
Balance Rock *(Pillsbury State Park)* Date: _____	
The BOB *(Concord)* Date: _____	
Boulder Natural Area *(Pawtuckaway State Park)* Date: _____	
Buffalo Rock *(Bow)* Date: _____	
Dog Rock *(Candia)* Date: _____	
Elephant Head Rock *(Crawford Notch)* Date: _____	
Frog Rock *(New Boston)* Date: _____	
Indian Rock *(Bedford)* Date: _____	
Sheep (Dog) Rock *(Hooksett)* Date: _____	
TMNT Rock *(Auburn)* Date: _____	

Optional Hikes/Drive Ups (pick 5)
A mix of difficult hikes and drive ups.

	Comments
Big Rock Caves *(Mt. Mexico)* Date: _____	
Eunice "Goody" Cole Rock *(Hampton)* Date: _____	
Gilfillan Rock *(Concord)* Date: _____	
Glen Boulder *(Randolph)* Date: _____	
Goodrich Rock *(Waterville Valley)* Date: _____	
Humongous Boulder *(Stoddard)* Date: _____	
Monkey Rock *(New Boston)* Date: _____	
Old Man of Keene *(Keene)* Date: _____	
Papoose Rock *(Lyme)* Date: _____	
Playscape Playground *(Highland Center)* Date: _____	

(Continued on next page)

Optional Hikes/Drive Ups (continued)

	Comments
Quimby's Pillow *(Mt. Moriah)* Date: _____	
Sarcophagus *(Mt. Monadnock)* Date: _____	
Tippin' Rock *(Swanzy)* Date: _____	
T-Rex Rock *(Manchester)* Date: _____	
Underhill's Chair *(Isle of Shoals)* Date: _____	
Wolf Rock *(Mason)* Date: _____	
Other Comments	

Congratulations on completing the NH Rocks That Rock 25!

To get your Patch Quest application, send an email to rocksthatrock25@gmail.com.

CPSIA information can be obtained
at www.ICGtesting.com
Printed in the USA
BVHW051752040921
616039BV00006B/20